FORGIVENESS AND REGRET

A COMPARATIVE ANALYSIS

SUSHMITA DUTTA

Published by True Sign Publishing House
Address: SY. No. 21/2 & 21/3, Sonnenahalli,
Krishnarajapura, Bengaluru,
Karnataka - 560049 India
E-mail: truesignbooks@gmail.com
Website: www.truesign.in

Forgiveness And Regret
A Comparative Analysis

Author: Sushmita Dutta

ISBN:978-93-5805-631-0

First Edition: 2023

CONTENTS

INTRODUCTION

Who hasn't been hurt by the actions or words of another person? Perhaps your parents' constantly criticized you growing up, a colleague damaged a project or your partner had an affair. Or maybe you've had a traumatic experience, such as being physically or emotionally abused by someone close to you. These wounds can leave lasting feelings of resentment, bitterness and anger — sometimes even hatred.

But if you hold on to that pain, you might be the one who most dearly pays for it.. By embracing forgiveness, you can also embrace peace and hope. Consider how forgiveness can lead you down the path of physical, emotional and spiritual well-being.

What is Forgiveness?

Forgiveness means different things to different people. But in general, it involves an intentional decision to let go of resentment and anger.

The act that hurt or offended you might always be with you. But working on forgiveness can lessen that act's grip on you. It can help free you from the control of the person who harmed you. Sometimes, forgiveness might even lead to feelings of understanding, empathy and compassion for the one who hurt you.

Forgiveness doesn't mean forgetting or excusing the harm done to you. It also doesn't necessarily mean making up with the person who caused the harm. Forgiveness brings a kind of peace that allows you to focus on yourself and helps you move on with life.

What is Regret?

Have you ever done something, said something, or not done something that you regret? You're not alone. Everyone has regrets about things in life. The question is, what can we do about it? How do we live a life with fewer regrets and how do we deal with the regrets we already have?

Regret is a self-focused negative emotion about something that has happened or been done by us. We feel bad because we did or didn't do something we believe we should or shouldn't have done. It involves acknowledging our role in our present circumstances, it also often includes self-blame.

CHAPTER 1

WHAT ARE THE BENEFITS OF FORGIVING SOMEONE?

Forgiving grudges and bitterness can make way for improved health and peace of mind. Forgiveness can lead to:

- Healthier relationships.
- Improved mental health.
- Less anxiety, stress and hostility.
- Fewer symptoms of depression.
- Lower blood pressure.
- A stronger immune system.
- Improved heart health.
- Improved self-esteem.

Why is it so easy to hold a grudge?

Being hurt by someone, particularly someone you love and trust, can cause anger, sadness and confusion. If you dwell on hurtful events or situations, grudges filled with resentment and hostility can take root. If you allow negative feelings to crowd out positive feelings, you might find yourself swallowed up by bitterness or a sense of injustice.

Some people are naturally more forgiving than others. But even if you tend to hold a grudge, almost anyone can learn to be more forgiving.

What are the effects of holding a grudge?

If you struggle with finding forgiveness, you might:

- Bring anger and bitterness into new relationships and experiences.
- Become so wrapped up in the wrong that you can't enjoy the present.
- Become depressed, irritable or anxious.
- Feel at odds with your spiritual beliefs.
- Lose valuable and enriching connections with others.

CHAPTER 2

HOW DO I MOVE TOWARD A STATE OF FORGIVENESS?

Forgiveness is a commitment to change. It takes practice. To move toward forgiveness, you might:

- Recognize the value of forgiveness and how it can improve your life.
- Identify what needs healing and who you want to forgive.
- Join a support group or see a counsellor.
- Acknowledge your emotions about the harm done to you, recognize how those emotions affect your behavior, and work to release them.
- Choose to forgive the person who's offended you.
- Release the control and power that the offending person and situation have had in your life.

What happens if I can't forgive someone?

Forgiveness can be hard, especially if the person who hurt you doesn't admit wrongdoing. If you find yourself stuck:

- Practice empathy. Try seeing the situation from the other person's point of view.
- Ask yourself about the circumstances that may have led the other person to behave in such a way. Perhaps you would have reacted similarly if you faced the same situation.
- Reflect on times when others have forgiven you.
- Write in a journal, pray or talk with a person you've found to be wise and compassionate, such as a spiritual leader, a mental health provider, or an impartial loved one or friend.
- Be aware that forgiveness is a process. Even small hurts may need to be revisited and forgiven again and again.

Does forgiveness guarantee reconciliation?

If the hurtful event involved someone whose relationship you value, forgiveness may lead to reconciliation. But that isn't always the case.

Reconciliation might be impossible if the offender is unwilling to communicate with you. In other cases, reconciliation might not be appropriate. Still, forgiveness is possible — even if reconciliation isn't.

What if the person I'm forgiving doesn't change?

Getting another person to change isn't the point of forgiveness. It's about focusing on what you can control in the here and now. Think of forgiveness more about how it can change your life by bringing you peace, happiness, and emotional and spiritual healing. Forgiveness can take away the power the other person continues to have in your life.

What if I'm the one who needs forgiveness?

The first step is to honestly assess and acknowledge the wrongs you've done and how they have affected others. Avoid judging yourself too harshly.

If you're truly sorry for something you've said or done and want forgiveness, consider reaching out to those you've harmed. Speak of your sincere sorrow or regret. Ask for forgiveness without making excuses.

You can't force someone to forgive you. Others need to move to forgiveness in their own time. Remember, forgiveness is a process. Whatever happens, commit to treating others with compassion, empathy and respect.

CHAPTER 3

HOW TO FORGIVE YOURSELF AND LET GO OF REGRETS?

We often hear the phrase "treat yourself" throughout the year, but we hear it considerably more around the holidays. Treating yourself to tangible things might increase your happiness for a brief amount of time, but it's important to know that we can also find meaning in things that will boost our self-esteem.

The best way to boost your self-esteem and reduce stress is by learning how to forgive yourself. By being forgiving of yourself, you can then accept yourself and be more responsible for your life choices. Self-forgiveness is the willingness to believe that you are worthy of love, respect, and great success. There are dangers when we fail to forgive, and these dangers might have the potential to limit our relationships with others and ourselves. A failure to forgive yourself might have the same consequences as holding grudges on others. Grudges or regret might lead to emotional bondage, uneasiness in your spirit, and induce uncertainty surrounding your relationships.

Forgiving yourself can be a difficult experience, as we tend to hold ourselves to higher standards. The act of self-forgiveness changes the energy and the physical structure of your cells and DNA. When you experience guilt, it can begin to close off important systems in your body that are responsible for healing. Guilt and regret are both very powerful emotions that represent feelings of resentment and might lead to self-punishment. The lack of forgiveness is emotionally and physically damaging.

When you have a hard time forgiving yourself it might lead to emotional, mental and physical damage. Sometimes the most difficult person to forgive is the one you face in the mirror. Some common emotions that challenge self-forgiveness are feelings of unworthiness, unresolved trauma, focusing on the past, placing blame on yourself, fear of failure and regret.

The past cannot be changed, and the future depends on the decisions you make today.

Here are some ways you can help yourself in the journey of forgiveness:

Acceptance.

Acknowledge that you are a human and know that every human makes mistakes. You are not a bad person, but one that needs grace and forgiveness. Take responsibility for your own healing.

Learn from mistakes.

Try to learn from your mistakes. Take the time to focus on the message, and understand the lesson being shared with you. Mistakes are an opportunity for growth.

Take risks.

Be willing to take risks. Try something new to help you find yourself again. Seek methods like therapy to channel your feelings. This will help you process and begin to move forward.

Visualize the future.

Visualize yourself free from guilt, regret and self-condemnation. Start by setting goals with your healing process. Visualize what your life would look like if you were free from regret.

Be intentional in new and improved decisions that might begin to open up opportunities for forgiveness and a happier future. Take time for yourself and your own healing.

CHAPTER 4

WHAT DOES IT MEAN TO REGRET SOMETHING?

If we say we regret something, it means that we disagree with our past decision-making. Maybe we decided not to take an opportunity that would have benefited us. Or, maybe we decided to break up with a romantic partner that we miss. Based on what we know now, our past decisions seem like the wrong ones.

What is the opposite of 'regret'?

The opposite of regret may involve a feeling of remorselessness and satisfaction over having made, what we believe to be, the right decision. Maybe the airplane we were supposed to get on crashes, and we feel an overwhelming sense that the decisions we made were correct. Or, maybe we break up with our romantic partner and quickly meet the love of our life. Overall, we see how our past decisions paved the way for what we really want.

What causes regret?

A recent study aimed to see what the most common causes of regret are:

- Education
- Career
- Romance
- Parenting
- Self-improvement
- Leisure

Less frequently reported regrets included: finance, family, health, friends, spirituality and community.

More specifically, people say they regret things like:

- Missed educational opportunities
- Failure to seize the moment
- Not spending enough time with friends and family
- Missed romantic opportunities
- Rushing into something too soon
- Unwise romantic adventures

Opportunity breeds regret

Ironically, the more opportunity one experiences, the greater chance for regret. If opportunities are denied or out of reach, we may experience anger or frustration, but not usually regret. The situation is out of our hands. But when we are given opportunities, that puts the onus on us—it's up to us to take advantage of these opportunities. Researchers speculate that this is the reason why education is something many people regret—we can always go back to school, so it's easy to regret not doing it .

More options, more regret

In the modern world, we have a zillion options for everything. More options often lead to more regret. Instead of enjoying the things that we have, we are aware that there are many other options that we didn't choose, and this gives us more chances for regret. For example, we might think, "Why did I buy this pair of pants instead of those ones?" "Why did I decide to get in a relationship with this person when I might meet someone better on a dating app?" This paradox of excessive choice actually makes us less happy and more regret prone.

How long does regret last?

Regret is not time-limited. We can experience it immediately or at just about any time later. For example, we might feel instant regret when we accidentally say something to a friend that hurts their feelings. Or, we might feel regret a short bit after the event. For example, maybe we get a test in a class and see that we haven't got the grade we desired. Then, we might regret not studying harder. Or, regret can even be pushed out . Maybe we dropped out of school and years later we are dragging ourselves to a thankless job when we suddenly feel regret; maybe we made the wrong decision to quit school.

What are we most likely to regret?

The research shows that action (versus inaction) produces more regret in the short term. For example, we might feel regret for saying something embarrassing or agreeing to do an annoying task for someone else. But these experiences of regret pass rather quickly .

It turns out that the things we're most likely to regret are the things we didn't do. Regrets of inaction are stronger and persist longer than regrets of action. So if we feel we "should have taken that trip", "should have asked this person out", "should have gone to college", these regrets likely last longer than regrets of having done something we might rather have not done—things like we "shouldn't have come to this party", "shouldn't have taken this job", "shouldn't have gone a date with this person."

When we don't take action, our imagination fills in the blanks about how awesome the outcome could have been. This leads our minds to generate more regret as we compare what currently is with what could have been.

CHAPTER 5

WHAT ARE THE IMPACTS OF 'REGRET'?

Regret is a negative emotion that occurs when a person believes his or her past actions or behaviors, if changed, may have achieved a better outcome. Regret is often closely associated with feelings of guilt and shame. We often express the emotion of regret to others in the form of an apology.

In general, regret pushes us to change our actions. We recognize that we have made a poor decision and we don't want to make it again. So we change our behaviors in ways that hopefully bring improvement in our life circumstances.

Impact of age on regret

As we get older, the things we are likely to regret may change. For example, a college student may be more likely to regret romantic decisions or mistakes they made with friends. However, older adults are more likely to regret educational and career decisions . This difference likely just reflects the types of decisions we are making at different ages. A young person may be more focused on relationships while an older person may be more focused on career.

Luckily, our overall level of regret goes down as we get older. This may be because we have fewer opportunities . For example, as we get older we may have fewer romantic prospects and are more likely to be settled into a job, house, family, etc. There may be fewer big decisions that need to be made about life changes, therefore, leaving fewer opportunities for regret.

Another explanation for the decrease of regret as we age may be that we've experienced more regret in the past and we have learned from it. We used that regret as motivation to change our behavior in ways that lead to less regret later in life. We've made that mistake before, and we won't do it again.

Regret may be characterized by negativity about the past in general, or about a particular incident in the past. For example, a person might feel badly about the way he or she has spent his or her life and be burdened by regret. Alternatively, the person might just feel badly about a particular incident—such as yelling at his or her mother the last time he or she saw her—and feel regret about it.

Regret tends to be a long-lasting emotion, and people might say that they are burdened by feelings of regret that they cannot eliminate. However, regret can also be a short-lived feeling. For example, a child might regret tripping his or her sister and then quickly move past these feelings. The fact that regret is associated with the past, though, can make it particularly difficult to process because the actions that led to the regret cannot be changed.

How regret can be helpful?

Regret can be beneficial by helping the person experiencing it gain insight and improve future decision-making skills. Research from the last two decades theorizes that regret is an essential psychological construct related to decision-making, coping and learning.

Regret can also be helpful because it signals the need for a corrective action, which can push people into implementing that action. Under the right circumstances, this can be considered a beneficial consequence of regret.

Mental health and regret

Even though regret may bring positive change to one's life, regret is more commonly associated with the negative effects it can have on a person's happiness. Regret may lead to:

- A bias in one's decision-making, resulting in poor choices being made
- Anxiety caused by repeatedly thinking about the perceived better choice or behavior
- Chronic feelings of sadness and dysphoria
- Varying degrees of guilt
- Shame
- Anger

Regret can significantly impede happiness because regret often causes people to feel shame, sadness or remorse about decisions or the ways in which they have spent their lives. Sometimes regret can contribute to depression, but depression can also cause feelings of regret that were not previously there.

Therapy can be a useful tool to help you or someone you know cope with feelings of regret. When people spend years fixating on a regrettable choice they often need help to move past it, and seeking a therapist can help people talk through, understand, and move beyond regret.

CHAPTER 6

WHY YOU SHOULD 'FORGIVE AND FORGET'?

'Forgive and forget' is an oft-repeated phrase which gets uttered so often. When someone really hurts you, you may question whether you really want to forgive someone. But there are many reasons why it's sometimes better to forgive and forget, even if a part of you doesn't want to.

Given below are a few reasons.

1. Forgiveness doesn't condone their actions.

Forgiveness doesn't mean what happened was right, and it doesn't mean that person should still be welcomed in your life. Forgiveness just means that you've made peace with the pain, and you are ready to let it go.

"There was a reason you came together, and there's a reason you are moving apart," psychologist Danielle Dowling, Psy.D., writes at mbg. "Acknowledge the good, the bad, and the beautiful from your time together and know that it all served an important purpose in both of your lives."

2. Forgiveness is not for other people.

Forgiveness is not something we do for others - it's something we do for ourselves.

Not forgiving someone is the equivalent of staying trapped in a jail of bitterness, serving time for someone else's crime. "It's a mixture of anger, depression and blame. But most of all, the opposite of forgiveness is stagnation," psychologist Kristina Hallett, Ph.D., writes at mbg. "It's getting mired in an emotional place regarding a particular incident, and it prohibits future growth and discovery. ... There's a common saying: Not forgiving someone is like slowly poisoning yourself and secretly hoping the other person dies."

You make the choice to either dwell on the pain caused by others, or you can forgive and move on.

3. Forgiveness is a sign of strength.

Gandhiji once said, "The weak can never forgive. Forgiveness is the attribute of the strong." It takes a strong person to face pain head-on, forgive, and release it.

Hallett says, "Your ability to forgive someone often has little to do with that person or what they did." The Merriam-Webster defines forgiveness as 'to cease to feel resentment against an offender' or 'to give up resentment of or claim to requital.' It's an internal state of being, and it's not dependent on anyone but you. The only person in control of your thoughts, feelings, and actions—and the only one who can make a shift occur—is you.

4. We also deserve forgiveness.

Hallett points out that our inability to forgive others can stem from an inability to forgive ourselves. The lack of acceptance for others may even fuel a lack of acceptance for ourselves.

Others deserve forgiveness, just like we do.

5. Forgiveness is healing.

"When we hold onto a resentment, grievance, shame, guilt, or pain from the past, our entire body-mind suffers," Deepak Chopra has told mbg. "Ultimately forgiveness is a gift we give to ourselves. We can benefit from forgiving even if the person we forgive isn't aware of our feelings or is even no longer alive."

To forgive someone is the highest, most beautiful form of love. You might just find that you get a sense of peace and happiness in return.

6. You'll get a pretty sweet bonus.

If none of the above appeals to you, then you might want to take the advice of Oscar Wilde: "Always forgive your enemies. Nothing annoys them so much."

CHAPTER 7

'FORGIVE AND FORGET': A SHORT STORY BY PRIYANSHI SAXENA

'Some goodbye helps people to come close. Will they come back?'

This story is about a father (Samid) and his son (Ref). They were poor and lived in a small house made of woods and trees. They were close when Ref was a kid. His father worked all day and when he reached home he used to play and enjoy with his son. Whenever he left home Ref used to see off his father with a kiss.

One day in the morning, Samid was preparing munchies and Ref was sitting on the door seeing outside. Ref asked his father will I never go to school, I also want to study.

Samid asked him to come inside and have some breakfast but Ref angrily shouted at him and went outside. Samid was very late so he covered the food and left for work.

Later in that evening when he reached home he saw that Ref was not there. He asked the neighbors for Ref but no one had any clue. He searched for him but found him nowhere. He came home at night and lay down. After sometime he thought for a while and left for the police station.

The police refused to file a complaint as they thought that he would come back in a few days. When 3 days passed and there was no clue, Samid again went to the police station and requested to file a complaint and start searching for his son. The police started taking this matter seriously and asked for any photo of him.

When Samid came home he saw a crowd in front of his home. When he went closer he saw that Ref was lying dead inside. His neighbors doubted Samid but didn't say anything. Someone from the crowd called the police.

When the police arrived they saw the body but couldn't find Samid there. The body was brutally disfigured and unrecognizable. The police sent the body for autopsy and searched for Samid.

A few months passed but there was no sign of Samid. The police kept on searching for Samid. They asked the neighbors but couldn't find any clue.

As the relations between the neighbors and Samid were not good, no one knew about Samid much.

When the police asked about the background of Samid, one of the neighbours told that no one knew about him much.

The police asked how you all know nothing about him? Was he new to this place?

Then one of them told, "No, no sirji, he is not new but he never spoke anything to us. His wife was killed years before and since then he and his son lived here. He used to go out for work all day and at evening when he returned he cooked food and played with his son. He never fought with anyone "

The police asked," Who killed his wife? When was his wife killed? Since when is he living here!? "

Then the one person who spoke before said that is all they knew. Samid told them only this much.

The police left from there. The constable who was sitting next to the police said," Sir, it seems like the one who killed his wife now killed his son and kidnapped Samid. So now we should find Samid and close the case." The police asked to stop the car on the roadside and asked the others to go to the police station and keep the complaint file on his table. And he left hurriedly after saying his sentence.

After 2 hours he reached the police station and asked for the complaint files. One of the constable placed it on his table.

He re-read the complaint filed by Samid and then suddenly he asked about the autopsy report. When he couldn't find the autopsy report in the evidence room he went to the hospital and asked about the copy of the reports and the details of the child. He couldn't find anything. He asked from the doctors who were on duty. Doctor Mehra came from his cabin and said that, "When you left the body for autopsy, around 1 hour later, an old man came and took the body and when we refused he said that he will commit suicide there. He was creating a scene and so we called the police but your man came too late. Till then it was impossible for us to handle him and he took the body with him." The police said you should've called me as I am handling the case, why you dialed 100.

Doctor Mehra didn't answer the question and left saying, "I am sorry officer I have to go."

The police officer went to the security room of the hospital and asked about the recording of cameras installed in the hospital.

He saw that Samid took the body but he didn't create any scene. The police officer was clueless as to why did the doctor told about creating scene and all? Why was the doctor helping Samid?

He had no questions and decided to follow the doctor instead of asking him. Four-five days passed but the doctor went from home to hospital and from hospital to home.

The police officer again went to Samid's home to find any clue, he searched for a while and saw that a small part was looking like it was digged in the early days. He started to dig it and found that there was a gun and pictures of some ladies and a diary.

He took all that as part of evidence and left.

He asked a constable to look after Samid's house every time in informal.

The police officer went to his home and kept the diary on the table and went for a shower. When he came out he dressed and picked up the TV remote and sat to watch TV. He fall asleep while watching TV.

When he opened his eyes he saw that his house was full of water and the diary he took from the home of Samid was wet and the pages stuck and some of the pages torn. He searched for the leakage and found that there was no leakage but someone had opened all the taps of the house. When he searched for the other belongings he got from Samid's house he found out that the gun which he got was some plastic game gun. But he was so sure that when he saw the gun at Samid's home it was the real gun. He was clear in his mind that it was a trap.

He sat for a while and began to think about all the incidents, he tried to connect but couldn't. He saw at the pictures of ladies which he got inside the dairy.

He thought what if he could get any clue from these pictures so he went to the police station and asked other team members to search for the ladies.

The other day the town was full of posters and hoardings of the ladies. The newspaper got the news of the ladies.

After five days, an officer got a call from a manager of the seven star hotel. The officer arrived at the hotel in informals as manager and asked him to come as a guest in the hotel.

The officer went to the manager and asked for a room for 2 days and asked about the details about the hotel in a normal way. A person standing far from him was noticing him. The officer went near him and asked about the person. He was the staff of the hotel, the manager who called the police.

The manager behaved as if he knew the officer from a very long time so he said that he will go to the room to see the arrangements and took the key from the officer.

When they entered the room the manager said that, "One lady from the picture you published visits here regularly. I know her she always stays in room 111." The officer asked for more information and then the manager said, you can meet her she is in the hotel. Then the manager and officer left the room. The manager went to the desk and the officer went inside the room 111 as he had the duplicate key. Seeing the lady the officer hid himself and slowly he went near her and put the tape on her mouth and handcuffed her. She was frightened and started crying but the officer sat in front of her and said, "If you will cooperate then I will let you go otherwise sit like this. I just want to know about yourself and why your picture was with Samid?" The girl stopped crying and gestured the officer to open her mouth. The officer opened her mouth and asked the answer.

The girl (Aalvi) told the story that 5 years before she came in search of job alone and there she met a boy Karan who told her that she can be an intern under him and asked to do daily tasks for him. In the beginning he asked me to send parcels at the addresses. When I asked him about what kind of internship is this he told me that it is to check your patience and honesty and will to do the work. I never questioned again as I was in need of the job but one day when I reached my home few men were there who kidnapped me. Next thing I remember is I found myself in a dark room and slowly I found that Karan was the leader of sex trafficking and he send me there, he sold me there, he told me that I will earn a good money now. I refused him but he didn’t listen to me. And there were few more girls. There was a guard, Samid bhaiya, he was nice he always tried to help but he couldn't do anything.

One day he tried to help us and many of the girls ran away and Samid bhaiya took his whole family away from there as it was dangerous to keep his family there.

Somehow the gang recovered the truth and threatened Samid bhaiya to bring back all the girls otherwise they would sell their daughter and wife.

One day Samid bhaiya was drunk when the members of the gang approached Samid bhaiya and asked if he bought any of the girls back. Samid bhaiya argued and screamed at them as he was not in his senses. The gang took her daughter and Samid bhaiya couldn't do anything. His wife was angry at him and asked him to bring back her daughter but Samid bhaiya killed his wife as he was so drunk that he could not sense himself. Before dying Samid's wife told her that she was not going to forgive him and not let him forget any of this. After that he went away with his son and never came back. We are not in contact of him now.

The officer understood the story and asked where is Karan now and from where he did his business.

Now with the help of Aalvi he found the place from where Karan worked and arrested him along with his gang and released the ladies.

The officer went to Doctor Mehra to ask about why was he helping Samid, then the doctor said that I am Aalvi's father and Samid had helped her so he was helping Samid as Samid was not guilty. Samid befooled everyone by the death of his son because someone from Karan's gang was following him to kill his son. And by faking the news of his son's death no one would follow him and he would be safe and the body you found in the house was fake. Samid is safe and so is his son.

Source: Reedsy

https://blog.reedsy.com › short-story › wvyrra

CHAPTER 8

WHY YOU SHOULD 'FORGIVE' BUT NEVER 'FORGET'?

We've all heard the proverb "forgive and forget" when someone has wronged us. The idea is that this will help keep peace, preserve relationships and maintain a calm mind.

Sounds good, but can you really do that — forgive an offense and then forget about it? And is that the best action to take?

Because this advice has been handed out for ages, you might think it's rooted in deep wisdom, and it must be easy to do.

Wisdom? Yes, in part. Easy? No, definitely not.

This proverb that we're all so familiar with might be more properly phrased as, "forgive, but don't forget."

What does it mean to forgive but not forget?

Knowing how to forgive someone can be an essential life skill. It can save friendships, restore faith in our kids and keep romantic relationships intact.

A 2015 study suggests that there are two types of forgiveness:

- **decisional forgiveness**: making a conscious decision to let go of hurt feelings, such as anger and resentment, putting them in the past, and moving forward free of the effects those feelings can bring
- **emotional forgiveness**: replacing negative emotions toward the person who has wronged you with positive ones such as sympathy, compassion, or empathy

Experts in this study suggest that emotional forgiveness can lead to higher levels of forgetting than decisional forgiveness or no forgiveness.

A 2021 study also suggests that forgetting is easier with emotional forgiveness than decisional forgiveness or no forgiveness.

But does forgiving someone require that you forget what they've done? Not necessarily.

"Forgiving and forgetting" implies that you've moved on and no longer think about the offensive act. But forgiving an offense can be hard to do.

A 2011 study suggests that forgiveness may give the person permission to continue the offense. In some cases, people who hurt others can manipulate the forgiveness process.

When "forgetting" what has been forgiven is challenging, learning from the experience may help some people cope if they encounter that behavior in the future.

Still, "forgiving and forgetting" isn't always possible in every situation. While some can learn from the experience, others may forgive to release the past and accept that what happened wasn't their fault and that no behavior could have changed it.

Is it possible to forgive and not forget?

If you don't forget, can you really forgive? It can be difficult to truly forgive someone when you know how they've hurt you.

But no one said that forgiveness was easy. It may be extremely hard. Forgiveness may be as much for you as it is for the person to whom you're granting it.

Forgiveness may help release emotional baggage, such as anxiety, anger and pain. A 2019 study notes that several studies have linked forgiveness to lower levels of depression and anxiety.

It also notes that forgiveness may even improve physical health and pain, while unforgiveness may increase heart rate and blood pressure.

The study of nearly 1,000 women ages 18 to 40 found that those who emotionally forgave an offense held the person less responsible for the offense than those who decided to forgive.

Practicing forgiveness may improve your emotional health and overall happiness, according to a 2016 review.

The Mental and Physical Health Benefits of Forgiveness

If you're still having trouble forgiving, especially when you can't forget, there may be some good reasons to continue trying.

- Forgiving is critical for our emotional well-being. By refusing to forgive someone, you may be holding on to all the anger and pain that their actions might have created. This can take an emotional and physical toll. According to a 2016 study, practicing forgiveness might help reduce stress, anxiety, and the likelihood of depression.
- We don't forget — we learn. Each experience teaches us something, even the painful ones. Forgetting means you're forgoing the lesson and growth that can come from it. Instead, consider using it to better equip you for the future.
- Forgiving strengthens relationships. All relationships have the potential to deepen and thrive because of what occurred. A 2011 study suggests that forgiving your partner may be crucial to maintaining a healthy romantic relationship. Forgiving may encourage you to become more committed to not allowing divisive and hurtful conflicts to occur in the future.
- Forgiveness has a positive effect on your physical health. Have you heard the phrase, "Being eaten up inside"? Holding on to resentment and anger can indeed create problems within your body. Those festering feelings can increase blood pressure and inflammation leading to potential heart problems.

Tips for how to forgive without forgetting

Convinced but unsure of how to start? You're not alone. If you're having trouble figuring out how to begin the process, consider the following tips:

- Identify and articulate the things you'd like to forgive. Too often, hurts and offenses get intertwined and knotted up. They may not even come from the same source. To start the process, try to be specific about what you'd like to forgive.
- Understand forgiveness. Forgiveness is a process and requires effort and patience.
- Acknowledge forgiveness. Try to think about what forgiveness will do for you, not for them.
- Forget about forgetting. It's not really possible to forget, nor is it necessary.
- Find perspective. This may require putting some distance between you and someone else, talking with a friend or family member, or even seeking counseling.
- Be ready to repeat the process. It can take more than one try to reach the point of being able to forgive.

Forgiveness is an important skill, and it can be positive. It may improve both your mental and physical health and lead to resolution and personal growth in some cases. And even though you've forgiven someone, it doesn't mean you have to forget their offense. Forgiveness is a process that can take time and may require some effort.

If you want help, consider reaching out to a mental health professional for guidance. They can help you with the next steps and provide you with tools to cope with your circumstances. "Forgiving and forgetting" is a choice, and if you choose not to do either, that's OK.

CHAPTER 9

DIFFERENCE BETWEEN 'FORGIVING' AND 'FORGETTING.'

"Some people think it's holding that makes one strong. Sometimes it's letting go." Unknown

I will never forget the moment my marriage ended. My husband and I had fought the night before, about many of the same things we'd been fighting about for the entirety of our four-month marriage.

He was dissatisfied with our sex life and my lack of respect for him. I was struggling with bipolar disorder, changing medications, going back to school, and trying to please a man who seemed to find fault with everything I did.

During that fight, he choked me twice to prevent me from screaming and running away. I learned quickly that if I didn't want to die, I would have to go limp, submit to his power, and hope he would release me from my position, pinned face down in our bed.

When I woke up the next morning, my spirit was broken. I felt as if I had a terminal disease. I knew with great certainty that I would die at the hands of my husband, I just didn't know how long it would take.

When my husband woke later, he wasn't satisfied with my newly submissive attitude. Another fight ensued, but this time, he used a different tactic. He insulted me, cutting me to the core with a comparison to a person who had caused me a great deal of pain and anguish.

As it turned out, my spirit had not been fully broken. The tiny scraps that remained rallied together to propel me out the door of our apartment. I ran screaming down the street like a mad woman, banging on a stranger's door and calling a friend to activate an escape plan.

I collected my dog, moved back in with my mother, and got a lawyer. Our divorce took seven months, almost twice as long as our marriage lasted.

And for the next year and a half after leaving him, I carried around the story of the violence and pain of our short time together like a security blanket.

Sometimes I would be angry with him.

I would wonder what was going through his head when he decided to cover my mouth and nose with one hand and immobilize my arms with his other free arm. I would cry when I compared the gentle, artistic soul I had fallen in love with to the invincible foe I faced at the end.

Sometimes I would blame myself.

If only I had been more polite, more respectful, been more generous in bed. If only I had bought him another truck, since the first two hadn't been adequate proof of how much I loved him. If only I had cut contact with my oldest and dearest friends sooner.

If only I hadn't sought solace and companionship at a local church. If only I had been able to listen unquestioningly to his demands, instead of arguing for silly things like access to psychological care and food and sleep.

If only I had been perfect, he wouldn't have choked me.

After a year and a half of this mental and emotional racket running through my head and heart on a daily basis, I finally started to see rays of light shining in through the cracks.

Reading **Tiny Buddha** had a lot to do with it, but the real breakthrough came when I took a road trip to a city I had never been to before, a city my ex-husband had visited before we were married.

Walking around in this city, I looked for the things he told me about. There was the bookstore, where he bought me a card. There was the burrito restaurant. There were the murals he admired.

Suddenly I was able to see my ex-husband in a much more sympathetic light.

He did not wake up one morning and decide that he was going to terrorize me. He did not set a goal of choking the woman he married. He was not a sociopath who enjoyed inflicting pain upon me.

He simply acted on his experiences and emotions, and chose to do what seemed logical at the time. Which is exactly what I had done, what we all do.

Looking back on it, I could see what a mess we were. Our insecurities and flaws became more exaggerated when we were together. We truly brought out the worst in each other.

In that moment, I decided to forgive my ex-husband. I bought a tiny carved elephant, one of his favorite animals, from the bookstore he had described to me, and took it down to a riverfront park. There, by the water, I said aloud everything I had just realized.

I apologized for not knowing myself better, and thereby not realizing how wrong we were for each other.

I apologized for not seeing my ex-husband for who he was, instead super-imposing my own fantasy onto him.

I thanked him for all of the good times—the road trips, the conversations, the paintings he gave to me, the way he encouraged my singing and guitar playing.

I wished for him to find health and wholeness.

I forgave him.

I placed the little elephant on a ledge overlooking the water, and walked away. The lightness of heart that I felt—the relief, the gratitude—all settled over me like the first snow on a pine branch.

And I realized as I drove away that forgiving and forgetting are very different things.

I can never forget the way his hands felt covering my face. I can never forget the panic of not being able to breathe. Nor should I strive to.

I must not forget the lessons I learned from my marriage.

I must not forget what is most important to me—freedom of movement, freedom to pursue friendships, freedom from fear and control. And I must not forget the warning signs I saw in my ex-husband, which I ignored, that almost cost me my life.

Although I forgave my ex-husband, I will not forget the harm we did to each other. And this is a good thing. If I forgot, I might walk into another similar situation. In remembering, I am able to evaluate new relationships and make sure I'm not going to re-make the same movie with different actors.

For too long, I resisted forgiving because I had confused "forgiveness" with "approval." Nothing could be further from the truth.

I don't condone my ex-husband's actions. But he is far from the only person in the world who has done something hurtful without intending to.

We have all hurt people in our lives, and we have all benefited from someone's forgiveness.

How bleak the world would be if everyone held onto their pain the way I did.

How bright the world can be when we release the burden of anger and resentment, and instead forgive.

And how beautiful the world can be when we learn from our pain instead of wallowing in it.

CHAPTER 10

HOW TO 'FORGIVE' YOURSELF?

Forgiveness is often defined as a deliberate decision to let go of feelings of anger, resentment, and retribution toward someone who you believe has wronged you. However, while you may be quite generous in your ability to forgive others, you may be much harder on yourself.

Everyone makes mistakes, but learning how to learn from these errors, move on and forgive yourself is important for mental health and well-being.

Discover why self-forgiveness can be beneficial and explore some steps that may help you learn how to forgive yourself?

How to 'Forgive' yourself?

Self-forgiveness is not about letting yourself off the hook, nor is it a sign of weakness. The act of forgiveness, whether you are forgiving yourself or someone who has wronged you, does not suggest that you are condoning the behavior. To forgive yourself, you should:

- Understand your emotions

- Accept responsibility for what happened
- Treat yourself with kindness and compassion
- Express remorse for your mistakes
- Make amends and apologize (including apologizing to yourself)
- Look for ways to learn from the experience
- Focus on making better choices in the future

Forgiveness means that you accept the behavior, you accept what has happened, and you are willing to move past it and move on with your life without ruminating over past events that cannot be changed.

The 4 R's of Self-Forgiveness

- Responsibility
- Remorse
- Restoration
- Renewal

Understand your emotions

Becoming aware of the emotions you are experiencing is an important part of learning to forgive yourself. Research has found that identifying and labeling your emotion can help reduce the intensity of your feelings. This can help you better regulate emotions, including those linked to feelings of guilt and shame.

Accept responsibility for your actions

Forgiving yourself is about more than just putting the past behind you and moving on. It is about accepting what has happened and showing compassion to yourself.

Facing what you have done or what has happened is the first step toward self-forgiveness. It's also the hardest step. If you have been making excuses, rationalizing, or justifying your actions in order to make them seem acceptable, it is time to face up and accept what you have done.

By taking responsibility and accepting that you have engaged in actions that have hurt others, you can avoid negative emotions, such as excessive regret and guilt.

Treat yourself with kindness and compassion

Forgiving yourself requires confronting your actions and showing remorse for what happened, but it is important to approach this with self-compassion. The key is to treat yourself with the same kindness that you would show to another person. Try to avoid being self-critical and instead be compassionate while still acknowledging that you made a mistake and want to do better in the future.

Express remorse for your mistakes

As a result of taking responsibility, you may experience a range of negative feelings, including guilt and shame. When you've done something wrong, it's completely normal, even healthy, to feel guilty about it. These feelings of guilt and remorse can serve as a springboard to positive behavior change.

While guilt implies that you're a good person who did something bad, shame makes you see yourself as a bad person. This can bring up feelings of worthlessness which, left unresolved, can lead to addiction, depression and aggression. Understand that making mistakes that you feel guilty about does not make you a bad person or undermine your intrinsic value.

Make amends and apologize

Making amends is an important part of forgiveness, even when the person you are forgiving is yourself. Just as you might not forgive someone else until they've made it up to you in some way, forgiving yourself is more likely to stick when you feel like you've earned it.

One way to move past your guilt is to take action to rectify your mistakes. Apologize if it is called for and look for ways that you can make it up to whomever you have hurt.

It may seem as if this portion of the process benefits only the person you've harmed, but there's something in it for you as well. Fixing your mistake means you'll never have to wonder if you could have done more.

Learn from the experience

Everyone makes mistakes and has things for which they feel sorry or regretful. Falling into the trap of rumination, self-hatred, or even pity can be damaging and make it difficult to maintain your self-esteem and motivation.

Forgiving yourself often requires finding a way to learn from the experience and grow as a person. To do this, you need to understand why you behaved the way you did and why you feel guilty. What steps can you take to prevent the same behaviors again in the future? Yes, you might have messed up, but it was a learning experience that can help you make better choices in the future.

Try to do better

Forgiving yourself also means making an active effort to do better in the future. As you approach similar situations, reflect on how you felt about your past mistakes. Rather than feeling guilty about those past errors, remind yourself about what you learned and how you can use that knowledge and experience to guide your actions going forward.

Limitations of 'Forgiving' yourself

While self-forgiveness is a powerful practice, it's important to recognize that this model is not intended for people who unfairly blame themselves for something they aren't responsible for.

People who have suffered abuse, trauma, or loss, for example, may feel shame and guilt even though they had no control. This can be particularly true when people feel they should have been able to predict, and therefore avoid, a negative outcome .

Benefits of 'Forgiving' yourself

The standard axiom within psychology has been that forgiveness is a good thing and that it conveys a number of benefits, whether you have experienced a minor slight or have suffered a much more serious grievance. This includes both forgiving others as well as yourself.

Mental Health

Letting go and offering yourself forgiveness can help boost your feelings of wellness and improve your image of yourself. Numerous studies have demonstrated that when people practice self-forgiveness, they experience lower levels of depression and anxiety. Similarly, self-compassion is associated with higher levels of success, productivity, focus, and concentration.

Physical Health

The act of forgiveness can also positively impact your physical health. Research shows that forgiveness can improve cholesterol levels, reduce bodily pain, and blood pressure, and lower your risk of a heart attack.

Relationships

Having a compassionate and forgiving attitude toward yourself is also a critical component of successful relationships. Being able to forge close emotional bonds with other people is important, but so is the ability to repair those bonds when they become fraught or damaged.

One study found that both parties benefit from the "offending partner" showing self-forgiveness. Specifically, both partners tended to feel more relationship satisfaction and have fewer negative thoughts about each other as a result of genuine self-forgiveness.

Challenges in 'Forgiving' yourself

So what is it that makes self-forgiveness so difficult at times? Why do people often continue to punish and berate themselves over relatively minor mistakes? Engaging in actions that are not in line with our own values or self-beliefs can lead to feelings of guilt and regret—or worse, self-loathing.

Some people are just naturally more prone to rumination, which can make it easier to dwell on negative feelings. The fact that self-forgiveness involves acknowledging wrongdoing and admitting that you might need to change can make the process more challenging.

Lastly, people who are not yet ready to change may find it harder to truly forgive themselves. Instead, of admitting they might need to change, they might engage in a sort of pseudo-self-forgiveness by simply overlooking or excusing their behavior.

Potential drawbacks of forging yourself

While self-forgiveness is generally thought of as a positive action that can help restore the sense of self, there is also research indicating that it can sometimes have a detrimental effect. The major pitfall of self-forgiveness is that it can sometimes reduce empathy for those who have been hurt by your actions.

Although self-forgiveness often relieves feelings of guilt, there are times this inward focus may make it more difficult to identify with others. You can avoid this by consciously practicing empathy with those who have been affected by your actions.

How do I let go of 'Guilt' and 'Forgive' myself?

Letting go of the guilt you feel often takes time. Focus on self-compassion, apologize if needed, and work on making amends. Instead of ruminating on feelings of guilt, focus on what you've learned and how you plan to do better going forward.

Why can't I seem to 'Forgive' myself?

There are a number of reasons why you might be struggling to forgive yourself. It might be because you're worried about making the same mistake again. Or perhaps you're worried about how facing your actions might undermine your self-image or damage your self-esteem. In such cases, taking gradual steps to truly change can be helpful. Talking to a mental health professional can help you process your feelings, develop new coping skills, and find ways to avoid the same mistakes in the future.

How do you 'Forgive' yourself for terrible things?

The more serious your mistake, the longer it may take to move past it. Regret can be normal, but it is important to take steps to move past it. You might feel grief about what happened, but it is important to allow yourself to feel and accept your emotions.

As you move forward, pay attention to the things you are doing to change and learn from the experience, and focus on the feelings of gratitude for what you've learned and the opportunity you have to keep trying.

CHAPTER 11

HOW TO LET GO OF GUILT AND PAST REGRETS?

'Forgive yourself. Let it go. Forget about it. Move on.' It's easy to say, but so much harder to actually do! We'll mess up sometimes, whether it's lashing out at a friend, engaging in self-destructive behavior, or cutting corners at work. And with those mistakes often come overwhelming feelings of guilt, shame, self-condemnation and humiliation.

Many counselors have found that these emotions can lead to stress, depression, anxiety and even heart disease if ignored. Fortunately, if you learn how to forgive yourself and decide to let go of the guilt, you can circumvent these negative effects and live better.

What Is 'Forgiveness'? Why is it so important?

Forgiveness is a deliberate decision to let go of negative emotions toward yourself or another person. The negative emotions that you might experience prior to forgiveness include those mentioned earlier: guilt, shame, self-condemnation, humiliation, as well as resentment .

Forgiving mistakes is incredibly important to your well-being. Dr. Frederic Luskin at Stanford University reports that "learning to forgive helps people hurt less, experience less anger, feel less stress and suffer less depression. People who learn to forgive report significantly fewer symptoms of stress such as backache, muscle tension, dizziness, headaches, and upset stomachs. In addition, people report improvements in appetite, sleep patterns, energy, and general well-being."

Forgiving yourself and others allows you to release negativity and focus on a more positive future. It also enables you to improve relationships with those closest to you.

Why is self-forgiveness so hard?

Too often, we punish ourselves for past mistakes, as if we could somehow "make up" the wrong that we've done. We walk through each day feeling less-than. We call ourselves losers and no good. We live chained to our past, holding on to hurts and grudges. And though no one else may know about our secret pain, the negative emotions we feel gnaw away at our joy and satisfaction in life.

Counselors report that the hardest person to forgive is yourself. Not the friend who back stabbed you. Or the dad that wasn't there for you. Or even the ex who broke your heart.

Why? Because you know yourself and you live with yourself every day. Go figure.

How to embrace 'Forgiveness'?

1. Talk about it.

When it comes to the past, silence can be deadly. So stop pretending. Free yourself from the bondage of holding it all in and talk about what's tearing you apart inside. Express the emotions you feel to a counselor, mentor, or friend you can trust. Forgiveness starts with being honest and vulnerable about who you are... the good and the bad. So say what you need to say.

2. Be honest with yourself.

We tend to think, "If I just pretend it never happened, maybe it will all go away." Sounds nice... but it isn't true. Choose to break out of denial and be proactive. Be honest about how you've messed up and the consequences of your behavior.

3. Accept it for what it is.

As an imperfect person, you will make mistakes in life. Face it. You will hurt people sometimes. You will have regrets. It's part of living in a less-than-perfect world. But you have a choice.

Either your past will keep you in a rut of guilt and shame or you will accept it for what it is and experience the freedom to move on and enjoy the now. Self-acceptance is critical to your emotional health, so don't miss out!

4. Let go.

Don't hold on to guilt. You don't need to justify your past actions or try to prove yourself. Letting go of the past means burying it and giving up your right to engage in self-condemnation. Forgiveness is a choice but also a process. It's choosing to stop hating yourself or cutting yourself down and to start seeing yourself as a valuable human being. One of the first steps of letting go is to just get it out there.

Developing realistic expectations

Evaluate the expectations you set for you. Are they healthy? Or are they unrealistic?

If you find yourself never being able to measure up — no matter how hard you try — you may just need to change a few things in your approach to life. Healthy expectations are achievable and fulfilling, not draining and overwhelming.

CHAPTER 12

HOW TO 'FORGIVE AND FORGET'?

When someone has done you wrong and you just don't know how to handle it. Should you forgive them and act as if nothing has ever happened? Or should you shun them and cast them away from your life with no hope of ever returning?

That's why it's important to learn how to forgive and forget?

When someone has hurt you, you might have a wide range of responses. You might be furious right away, extremely sad, or you don't even want to deal with them at all.

These are all logical reactions to someone doing you wrong, but they don't exactly answer the question of whether you should forgive and forget someone when they hurt you *intentionally or unintentionally*. Neither do they help you decide the right step, or help you with how to forgive someone and eventually forget what they did to you.

Before we get into how to forgive and forget, you have to ask yourself a really simple question.

Do they deserve forgiveness?

There are so many people in the world who spend years contemplating this very question. Forgiveness is something that can take a lifetime for a person to accomplish. It doesn't come naturally to most of us.

1. They apologize right away

People who deserve forgiveness know their fault and acknowledge it right away. If they did something wrong and recognized it and showed you as much, then they should be forgiven-assuming their wrongdoing wasn't that bad. But then again, "sorry" just can't undo some things.

2. You found out from them

Not only is it important they apologize right away, but if they did something without your knowledge and are the first to tell you about it instead of some co-worker, you know they are really sorry.

They realized their mistake a little too late, but they still realized it and wanted to make it right as soon as possible. So if this is the case, then forgive them!

3. It was a minor mistake

Little things are much easier to forgive and forget than major ones. If they've done something just small enough then it's not a big deal, then forgiving them might even be the easiest option. By not letting the little things go, you turn them into huge issues causing a lot more harm than they originally were.

4. They've never done anything like it before

If this is the first offense for them and you know they're really sorry, just let it go. Make sure to communicate how much it hurt you, but forgive them. Everyone deserves a second chance.

5. You feel like you can still trust them

This is a point easily forgotten. If someone has lied or hurt you in any way, but, overall, you still feel like you can trust them 100%, you should forgive them.

Your gut instinct is usually right and maybe this person just slipped up.

6. You genuinely feel they're sorry

Just saying the words, "I'm sorry," doesn't do anything if you don't feel like they mean it. If you really believe they put forth the effort to apologize and make sure you know how sorry they are, then that's worth forgiveness.

7. What they did doesn't change your perception of them?

It's hard to forgive someone for something they did especially when it completely changes the way you view them as a person. Sometimes people do stuff so wrong and horrible in your mind you can't even imagine remaining in a good place with them.

But if what they did doesn't change your view and opinion of them as a person, it's safe to forgive them. As long as their actions still follow the rest of these guidelines on how to forgive and forget, that is.

8. You know right away you'll get over it eventually

It's okay to be angry with them. It's okay to tell them off and have a few words with them.

But if you know after the anger passes that it's something you'll get over fairly easily, it's worth forgiving them for.

9. They've made it up to you somehow

It doesn't have to be something fancy. But if they have somehow made an effort to make it up to you, they deserve your forgiveness.

It shows they are sorry enough to do something about it to make sure you forgive them. And for that, it's worth it.

'Forget' – How to decide if the pain caused is worth forgetting for good?

Forgetting when someone has wronged you is a whole different thing than simply forgiving them. Since we can't actually control what we remember, the term "forgetting" isn't exactly true.

A more accurate phrase would be "letting go" because if you forgive and forget, you are basically vowing to never reopen the incident for discussion. Here's how to know if you should not only 'forgive', but also 'forget' and let go of the issue for good.

1. You weren't that mad about it

They may have been situations where you wouldn't let it go because you thought you were supposed to be mad about it. Society as a whole would agree that what that person did was really bad.

But the truth is, you might not have been that angry. Maybe it's because you had already forgiven them. Or maybe it was because you just knew they didn't mean it. But either way, if it doesn't anger you that much, it's not worth holding onto.

2. It wasn't something horrible

Just like you should easily forgive the small things, forget the small things, too. There's no point in holding onto the little negative things in life. There are far too many bigger issues you should make space for in your mind.

3. You know they'll never do it again

If you know deep down there's no possibility of something like this repeating, just forget it. However, if it happens again even when you thought it wouldn't, hold onto that. Only forget if you're 100% sure they would never ever do something like that again. It'll make your interactions with them much easier if you wipe it out of your mind.

4. They've never done anything like this in the past

It is the first offense and it won't happen again. It doesn't seem like it's a habit, and you'll be safe just forgetting the whole thing ever happened.

5. You want to give them a second chance

It's almost impossible to give anyone a second chance when you didn't forget what they did in the first place. It isn't fair because you're not giving them a clean slate.

If you actually want them to have a second chance at proving themselves to you, then you owe it to them to forget their previous incident and truly give them that clean slate. So, in this instance, forgive and forget.

6. You know that you can

For some people, it's just too hard to forget about something when it hurt them. While this is understandable, it can really injure someone when they really do want to forget.

So, before you tell this person you forgive them and will forget about it, just make sure you can really forget it. Otherwise, you'll both run into issues when it's brought up in conversation down the road.

How to forgive someone – and forget, so you can have a better relationship with them?

Now that you know if you should simply forgive, or forgive and forget, how do you actually do this?

1. Work through your feelings

When someone hurts you, it's important to not try to bury your feelings. Instead, you should bring them out and feel them. Try to work through the anger and the grief the best you can. When you do this, you can process your emotions.

Then, after you do that, try to calm down and look at it objectively and logically. Sometimes, when you are overcome with emotion, you don't see things clearly.

2. Tell them what they did and how it affected you

Maybe the person doesn't even know that they hurt you. If that's the case, then you need to talk to them and tell them what they did and how it affected you. Their actions could have been accidental, but that doesn't mean that it hasn't changed you.

So, give them the respect to tell them how you were hurt by them. If they weren't sorry before, they will be once you tell them this and talk to them about it.

3. Think of it from their perspective

Most people are very self-centered. In other words, we only see things from our own perspectives. And sometimes, we expect everyone else to see the world the way we see it too. But that's not realistic.

Maybe you thought what they did is unacceptable. But was it really? Or are you the only one who thought it was unacceptable? Not everyone feels the exact same way you do. So, if you want to know how to forgive and forget, try to look at it from their perspective too, not just your own.

4. Are you responsible for anything?

It's so easy to blame the other person for hurting you. After all, they are the ones who took that action *or inaction,* right? But maybe you are partially responsible for how they acted too. Human relationships are very interdependent.

In other words, both people's actions affect the other person's actions. So, maybe there was something you did – or didn't do – that affected their behavior that hurt you. It's not easy to take personal responsibility, but you really should do it.

5. Don't take it personally

Many times, when someone hurts us we can't help but take it personally. But sometimes, what they did isn't directly about you. It's more about them and their problems.

For instance, let's say you are not getting enough love and affection from your partner. You might be angry and think it's because you're not attractive enough. But it could just be that they aren't an affectionate person. Their behavior isn't because of you, it's because of them.

6. Try not to judge too much

People love to be critical and judge others. This is unfortunate because no one is perfect. So, why would you expect people to be perfect and conform to all of your expectations? That's not reasonable.

So, if you want to forgive and forget, try to refrain from judging what they did too much. Of course, it might have been really bad and completely unacceptable. In that case, judge all you want. But if it's something relatively minor, then don't be too critical.

7. Accept what happened

When we hold back our forgiveness, it's almost like we won't let go of the hope that the past will change. But of course, you can't change the past. It happened. It won't magically disappear.

So, you just need to accept that you can't change it. One of Buddha's famous quotes says, "It is your resistance to what is that causes your suffering." In other words, you're resisting an unalterable past, and that is why you suffer.

8. Forgiving isn't condoning

A lot of people think that if they forgive someone, it's the same as condoning what they did. They think it's almost like saying to them, "What you did is alright, and go ahead and do it again to me!"

But that's not true. Just because you forgive doesn't mean that you are saying it's okay. You can forgive, but let them know that they should never do it again. And that you will probably never really forget.

9. Let it go for yourself

Buddha also has another great quote: "Holding on to resentment is like drinking poison and expecting the other person to die." In other words, resentment only hurts yourself, not the other person.

Carrying around negativity and resentment is a heavy burden. It's like carrying around a lot of luggage with you. It gets exhausting. So, you should let it go so you can feel lighter and happier, and that has nothing to do with them.

Knowing how to forgive and forget is not easy, but it can be done. The road to forgiveness can be a long and lonely one for some people. Make it easier on them and yourself by using this guide to learn when it's okay to forgive and when it's time to finally forget about the whole thing.

CHAPTER 13

HOW TO 'FORGIVE' YOURSELF WITH SELF-COMPASSION?

When someone hurts us, the process for forgiving them can be fairly straightforward. We learn this in school as children. You might talk about what happened and they share their experience. Or, you don't talk to them, but you gain some perspective and forgive them for the pain they caused you.

You weren't taught how to forgive yourself. As a result, you struggle to move on when you've let yourself down.

Forgiving others can feel much easier than forgiving ourselves. When we experience guilt, we often get trapped in a spiral of our own feelings. Instead of having that conversation with another person, we start listening to our inner critics — and they're not so forgiving.

Why is forgiving yourself so hard?

When someone else does something that hurts us, our reasons for holding a grudge are usually clear. We want the hurt to be acknowledged. Once they've apologized and made amends, we're usually clear to move on.

But when it comes to forgiving ourselves, things get much more difficult. When someone else hurts us, our anger can be self-protective. In a way, holding a grudge against them and demanding restitution keeps our self-image intact. When we're upset with ourselves, though, it's because we've violated our values in some way. Because of that, our feelings are usually more complicated than just anger. We're mad at ourselves, yes — but we're also disappointed and ashamed.

These feelings can be incredibly difficult to sit with. Most of the time, when we feel uncomfortable or painful, we try to push the feelings out of consciousness. This can become a habit that actually damages our self-awareness. It's really hard to be selectively self-aware, and avoiding the things that embarrass us - feels like a small price to pay for keeping our identities intact.

Sometimes, in order to avoid taking action or apologizing for our mistakes, we use our negative feelings as a shield. We think if we make ourselves feel bad enough, we can make up for whatever we did. Experiencing guilt can be very healthy and productive if we use it to gain insight into our behavior and values. When feelings of guilt turn into shame, however, it can stop us in our tracks.

We also tend to think that beating ourselves up shows how seriously we take our past mistakes. We tend to think that "letting ourselves off the hook" means that we haven't learned anything or that we take a careless approach towards our lives. Self-loathing is not a prerequisite for success. This kind of self-flagellation does nothing but fuel our inner critic.

What is an inner critic?

Our inner critic is the small voice inside that constantly tells that we're failing, we're doing something wrong, or that we should be better. It's super mean, to be honest. What's so bad about that critical voice is that it's meaner than we would ever be to a friend or loved one. And we certainly wouldn't tolerate someone saying those things to us (or about someone we love).

But when these thoughts stay inside, they sound much more credible. We tend not to question the thoughts that run through our minds because we tend to be less aware of them. This unconscious inner voice can do a lot of damage. And developing self-compassion is the only real way to shut it up.

How self-compassion supports self-forgiveness?

So what does self-compassion mean? Well, compassion — when directed towards others — means that we empathize with their struggles. We're able to imagine how another person feels, look kindly at their circumstances, and give their actions the benefit of the doubt.

What is self-compassion?

Self-compassion means that we treat ourselves just as gently as we would a friend. We recognize that we're feeling down, and are mindful about alleviating that pain. That might mean easing our expectations, doing something nice for ourselves, or validating our own emotions.

When we're self-compassionate, self-forgiveness comes much more easily. That's because we're able to put our failures into perspective. We recognize that while we may have disappointed ourselves in some way, it's not because we are inherently bad or incapable people.

Parents are often taught to separate their children from their behavior. Kids need to know that they are loved unconditionally, no matter what they do. Mindful parenting experts encourage parents to say "I don't necessarily love what you did, but I love you, and we can fix it."

This attitude of self-parenting can help us begin to develop self-compassion. Self-forgiveness is an action that we take to release the pain of an embarrassing or distressing situation. But self-compassion is a way of being. We can be compassionate with ourselves every single day, and we may find that we have less and less to forgive.

5 benefits of self-forgiveness

At its root, self-criticism is a protective mechanism. Its function is to save us from social and professional failures. Our critical voice is trying to keep us in line with our values.

Being critical can actually be counterproductive. Harsh criticism isn't really motivating — it's demoralizing. And it certainly doesn't put us in the position to learn from our mistakes and move forward in a constructive way.

Self-forgiveness, on the other hand, has many benefits — both internally and externally. Here are 5 benefits of forgiving yourself.

1. Improves emotional and mental health

Our negative thoughts can increase stress, anxiety, and depression. When we are compassionate with ourselves, we relieve the internal pressure of these negative emotions. Stanford University researchers write that "those who practice self-forgiveness have better mental and emotional well-being, more positive attitudes and healthier relationships."

2. Increases productivity

We all make mistakes. When we dwell on and try to minimize them we don't have the energy to learn from them and move on. Self-compassion improves our confidence, empathy, focus, and resilience.

3. Reduces cognitive dissonance

When we do something that feels "wrong," we feel psychological discomfort (known as cognitive dissonance). This feeling is a early warning that we're off course and out of step with our values. Navigating this feeling as a learning experience and a way to bring you back into alignment helps to reduce the negative effects of these internal contradictions.

4. Decreases impostor syndrome

When we let go of our need to be perfect, we can embrace a growth and learning mindset. This attitude of being an eternal student is fundamentally at odds with impostor syndrome. When you embrace that you're not perfect, you won't have such a hard time forgiving yourself for your mistakes. You'll see them as opportunities to grow as you keep moving forward — and they may even become your competitive advantage.

5. Improves your physical health

In addition to your mental health, letting go of guilty feelings has physical health benefits. A meta-analysis involving more than 26,000 participants showed strong correlations between forgiveness and overall health. The biggest improvements were in cardiovascular health, with noted reductions in pain, cortisol levels, and blood pressure.

What happens if you don't forgive yourself?

Sometimes, we get stuck in the story about what happened and it feels impossible to move on. There's a physical and emotional toll to being stuck in that space of non-forgiveness. It damages your self-esteem, your relationships, and your willingness to take risks. Your entire view of yourself becomes limited, filtered through the lens of "what you did wrong."

Learning to forgive is about letting go of the guilt and shame associated with the situation that's paining you. And it can be especially difficult when you feel that you've hurt someone else. You won't feel like you have the ability to forgive yourself while the other person is still hurt.

How to forgive yourself?

Here are some ways to kick start the forgiveness and healing process:

Ways to forgive yourself

- Understand that you're not perfect
- Get clear on why you're upset with yourself
- Repair what you can
- Find a way to close the door
- Regain perspective

1. Understand that you're not perfect

You're not perfect. Say it in the mirror, write it down, get it on a coffee cup. You're not perfect — and you're not a bad person, either. You're just a human being. Extend yourself the same grace that you extend to others. Are you expecting yourself to live up to standards you would never impose on anyone else?

2. Get clear on why you're upset with yourself

Try to uncover what's at the root of your guilty feelings. Is it perfectionism? Have you caused someone else pain? Have you done something that you're embarrassed about? Whatever it is is probably uncomfortable to look at, but taking it head-on can be educational.

Chances are, it's not hard to imagine someone else doing the same thing and being completely unbothered. For example, I get very unhappy with myself when I don't complete things on time. It's the number one thing I beat myself up about. Yet, I have friends that turn in everything late — or not at all — and could care less. And guess what? I don't think that they're bad people.

Try to be scientific about what happened and why it's bothering you so much. In my case, being late makes me feel irresponsible and incompetent. I don't like to think of myself as either of these things, and I don't want anyone else feeling that way either.

3. Repair what you can

Once you've identified what your "wrongdoing" is, you'll be able to tell if you need to make amends for it. You may owe someone an apology . Even if the ship has sailed and you'll never have a chance to make it up, you can acknowledge it for yourself so you can let go of the past. You're not a bad person, you just didn't finish something. It's not fun, but it happens.

4. Find a way to close the door

This is the most challenging part of self-forgiveness. Now that you've seen what your part in it is find some closure. Apologize, or not. Fix it, or not. But whatever it is, move on.

5. Regain perspective

When we get wrapped up in self-condemnation, it certainly feels that way. Talking to a friend really helped me to dig out of the guilt. I learned that no one was really as mad at me as I was. The good news about that was that I could always choose to cut myself some slack.

You're the only one who can forgive yourself.

In Buddhism, there's a saying: "Suffer what there is to suffer, and enjoy what there is to enjoy." When we get stuck on beating ourselves up, though, we suffer through it all. Learning to separate our selves from our circumstances can help us develop perspective and resilience. Once we stop suffering through our struggles, we can learn how to grow from them.

CHAPTER 14

HOW 'REGRETS' CAN HELP YOU MAKE BETTER DECISIONS?

Have you ever regretted something you did or didn't do in life? If you've lived a long life, you probably carry many regrets, large and small. Some of my own regrets relate to my career, past relationships and parenting . No matter the regret, it's hard not to wonder how things might have turned out if I'd only made a different—and better—choice at the time.

Ruminating on past mistakes can lead to depression or anxiety if it continues unabated. But a new book by psychologist Robert Leahy, **'If Only...Finding Freedom from Regret'**, suggests that regrets don't always have to bog you down. If you understand how regrets work, recognize their effect on your decision making, and find ways to manage life's inevitable disappointments, you can suffer less from regret and, instead, use your regrets as helpful guideposts for your life. "Regret is a part of life, but it doesn't have to take over and hijack you," he writes.

Nature of regret

Regret can come in different forms—for something we did (like overeating or hurting our loved one) or something we didn't do (like not graduating from college or not asking someone out on a date). Most people have a mixture of both types, though the latter tends to make us feel worse, writes Leahy.

According to research, the most common sources of regret involve our education, career, romance, and parenting . That's because we tend to regret things that reflect bigger concerns and opportunities in life, rather than what we ate for breakfast.

Culture can affect how people experience regret, too, with people from more individualistic cultures usually having more regrets about their personal situation (like achievement or career) and those in collectivist cultures having more regrets about their relationships. And women and men differ some in how they experience regret, with women typically regretting romantic relationships more than men and men regretting inaction more than action.

Regret is associated with unpleasant emotions, like sadness, disappointment, guilt, and shame. But people also regard it as one of the most beneficial negative emotions, because it can be instructive. For example, if we regret how we behaved the last time we drank too much, we're less likely to order a third round the next time we're at the bar. Or, if we regret yelling at our child when angry, we may take a breath the next time we're upset and respond with compassion.

Our regrets can teach us about ourselves, help us to avoid repeating mistakes, and encourage us to make better decisions in the future. On the other hand, if we use our regrets to beat ourselves up, or if we ignore them completely, they will not lead to growth. The key is finding the right balance, says Leahy.

"Regret doesn't have to lead directly to self-recrimination," he writes. But "never feeling regret is not a sign of wisdom or righteousness. It may be a sign you don't learn from your mistakes."

Why some people suffer from regret more?

Some of us are more prone to regret than others, and Leahy provides multiple questionnaires within his book to help you identify where you fall on that scale. Though there is no way to eliminate regret completely—and the world would be worse if we did—there are factors that increase our chances of experiencing regret in a more negative way and suffering from it, says Leahy.

Here are some of those risk factors.

Not tolerating ambivalence. Many life choices have pros and cons, and there are no guarantees about the future. But, if you can't stand uncertainty, you are bound to avoid making hard choices, leaving you vulnerable to later regrets.

Falling prey to biases. We all have cognitive biases, but some influence regret more than others. If you suffer a lot from negativity bias (or not even seeing the positives in your life), black-and-white thinking (thinking things are either all good or all bad), or catastrophizing (thinking that if something goes wrong, you won't be able to handle it), it's bound to affect how much you suffer regret.

Worrying about how bad we'll feel in the future. If you're the kind of person who often anticipates feeling awful for making a choice, it may keep you from deciding on a course of action that could bring you happiness, increasing the potential for regret.

Having too many choices. "Regret is an opportunity emotion—the more opportunity we see, the more likely we are to regret something," writes Leahy. For example, a college graduate with multiple job offers might regret taking one over another, especially if it doesn't pan out. Having too many choices increases your potential for making the "wrong" one.

Being a perfectionist. If you expect to have an ideal, happy life all of the time and are not easily satisfied, you will be more prone to regret. "Maximizers" (people who seek out optimal outcomes) tend to feel more regret than "satisficers" (people who are content with good-enough outcomes), unless they can take steps to lessen their maximizing tendencies.

How regret can guide our decisions?

"Regret is a possible element of any decision that we make," writes Leahy. "But the likelihood that you will regret your decisions will depend on how you think about making your decisions and how you cope with living with the result."

If you're someone who lets past regrets fester in your mind, Leahy recommends that you fight against irrational thinking and think more realistically about where you are in life. He suggests using approaches from cognitive-behavioral therapy to question your assumptions.

Here are some of his tips.

Remember that you don't know things would have turned out better. If you imagine your life would have been better "if only...," keep in mind that your assumption is not based on real evidence. Instead of focusing on where you might have been, turn toward the future and remember it can change based on the choices you make now.

Focus on the positive aspects of your current life, to balance out the negative feelings that come with regret. Your negativity bias can keep you preoccupied with what's wrong rather than what's right. So, it's a good idea to practice gratitude for the good in your life—even for the small, simple things.

Don't forget that sometimes things don't turn out the way you wanted them to, even with your most thoughtful planning. Life can hand you lemons, but that's not necessarily your fault. You cannot be omniscient; so, you need to accept that sometimes you will regret your choices. But that doesn't mean you should criticize yourself endlessly. Better to learn from your mistakes than to punish yourself.

Accept trade-offs and compromises. Not everything has to turn out just the way you wanted it to. You will limit your progress if you insist otherwise and make yourself miserable in the process. So, aim to be a satisficer rather than a maximizer.

Overall, Leahy advises that, once you've learned whatever lessons regret can teach you, you can let go of unrealistic expectations about what might have been, enjoy your life as it is, and start planning for a better future.

"Look around you at what is in the present moment and hold on to it with a warm embrace," he writes. "Because your regrets will only keep you from what you have and who you are and trap you in a fictional world that never was—and never could have been."

CHAPTER 15

HOW TO DEAL WITH 'REGRET'?

Imagine you're at a cocktail party where every person there is a past version of yourself. There's a children's play area with all the little versions of yourself. There's a TV room with your teenage selves watching music videos and playing video games. Then there's dozens of adult you's walking around, sipping whatever you drank when you were young and broke, representing each of the distinct periods of your life: the insecure college you, trying to look smarter than you actually are; the exhausted you from your first job; the doe-eyed and innocent you from the first time you fell in love.

Now, this might sound like fun. But I think this "Cocktail Party of You" would actually get quite boring. The reason is that for each version of you that you talk to, you know everything that they know, while they only know a fraction of what you know.

That's not to say it wouldn't be endearing. You'd hang out with your awkward teenage self and reassure them not to worry, those painful high school years will pass and things will get better. You'd talk to your arrogant 23-year-old self and compassionately bring them down . You'd talk to your smitten self who had just fallen in love for the first time and bask in the feelings of a new, young relationship—while not disclosing that Mr./Ms. Perfect is about to drag your heart across the pavement and smash it a dozen times with a hammer.

But then there'd be that one former self that you'd want to avoid... you know the one. That former self that did that horrible thing you've never quite found a way to forgive yourself for. If forced to finally speak to them, you would immediately start chastising them, "How could you? What were you thinking? You are such a moron, my god."

Then the cocktail party would be ruined. The cocktail party of you would collapse into this one pointed, awful moment in your life that would suck away the joy and vibrance of all the others.

The 'Cocktail Party of You' is a kind of metaphor for what happens when you experience regret. You abandon and neglect the celebration of all of the interesting parts of your life to hone in on this one festering mistake that haunts you.

'Regret' is a form of self-hatred. If who you are today is a culmination of all of the acts that have led up to this moment, then the rejection of some past act is. Therefore. a rejection of some part of you in this moment. Hating some part of yourself in the present messes you up psychologically. But hating a part of your past is not much different. It harbors shame and resentment. It inculcates self-loathing. And it makes you a real drag at parties, metaphorical and otherwise.

But the way to get over regret is not to ignore it. It's to push through it. It's to engage that former self, to talk to them directly and understand why they did what they did. It's to sympathize with that former self, to care for them, and ultimately, to forgive them.

Learning from your regrets

What's the difference between a mistake and a regret?

I would argue a regret is simply a mistake that we haven't learned the proper lesson from yet. Often, we regret because we did something so cataclysmic that it's difficult to learn the appropriate lesson. But often, we regret not because our actions were so heinous, but simply because we lack the imagination to pull some productive meaning out of them.

Learning from our mistakes is such a fundamental component of not being a shitty person, that I don't even know where to start. But let's put it this way: if you do something wrong, but you learn from it, then suddenly that mistake becomes helpful. Developing a habit of learning from our failures is like this magical elixir that transmutes all of the embarrassing cringey shit of our lives into making us better. And while that might not remove all our negative feelings, it certainly prevents things from getting worse.

Regret serves an adaptive purpose. It can help us or hurt us. When we feel regret, we can either wallow in our past mistakes or we can take steps to ensure we don't repeat our past mistakes.

The way you move on isn't by rationalizing all of these uncomfortable feelings away—by blaming yourself or the world for your misfortune—it's by accepting your mistakes, by understanding what happened and integrating that experience into your understanding of who you are today.

This forces you to take responsibility. and if you truly take responsibility , you don't repeat them—that is what regret is for.

Questioning your narratives

By learning how to question our narratives, we can gain greater perspective on how bad what we did actually was. And if we're honestly questioning ourselves, we'll often find that it wasn't nearly as bad as we thought.

For instance, let's say Timmy wasted his life savings in a pyramid scheme. Timmy feels awful. His wife hates him. His friends ridicule him. He can't pay his rent. Everything is falling apart.

In the moment, due to how painful the event is, Timmy constructs a narrative for himself, "I wasted all our money because I'm an idiot and I ruined our lives. If only I could go back and do it over again."

Timmy now has a regret.

What's dangerous about narratives like this is that they self-perpetuate. Our minds are meaning-making machines, and negative narratives are particularly pernicious. If Timmy believes he's a piece of shit and horrible with money, then whenever he has new experiences, he will interpret them through the "I am a piece of shit and terrible with money"9 lens. He will also interpret good things that happen to him as simply good luck, and bad things that happen to him as his own fault.

The problem with our narratives is that they are chronically short-term, emotional, and self-centered. What Timmy's narrative doesn't consider is that losing your money can have some subtle long-term benefits.

Listening to our worst hits album, on repeat

When we experience regret, we are choosing to relive our past. We are replaying our broken narrative over and over again. We are living as though the past is still true, even though it has long stopped explaining the world well for us, and even though the broken narrative continues to hurt us.

The problem is that we identify with these lost opportunities—we take these failures on as our lost identity, the person we should have been but never were. And then we torture ourselves with that idealized image.

Let's say you're in a dead-end job. And maybe you're not the young person you once were, so you think it's too late to do something different. You're too old to go back to school, too far into your career to change paths, and too settled in your life to make changes that will affect others, like your family.

So you have constructed this ideal self that reflects who you wanted to be 10, 15, or 20 years ago rather than who you are today.

Your ideal self is:

- Young, because that's when you're supposed to go to school;
- Single and responsibility-free, because that's when you're supposed to develop the foundation of your career.

I used to think I was going to be a musician. Then I dropped out of music school. I don't sit around thinking, "Oh man, if only I hadn't dropped out, I could have been a musician—what's wrong with me?" No, I realized that my desire to be a professional musician was a totally arbitrary ideal in my mind and I could change it.

The second reason this obsession over our idealized self is dumb is that even if you did somehow revitalize your sense of youth, it would probably require deluding yourself in some other harmful way.

Meanwhile, with each passing year, you get a little older and take on a few more responsibilities and you grow further and further away from this idealized youthful self. As it becomes less and less attainable in your mind, you feel your idealized self slipping away. And you regret it. You regret it so much—so much time lost, so much time wasted.

Let it die.

Instead, choose the right career as the older and wiser version of yourself now that you have an idea of what you actually want. Being older has so many advantages! Use them and move on.

By moving through your regrets and accepting the falsity of your ideal selves, you free yourself to take responsibility for the present.

Regrets and Responsibility

I've said before that in order to let go of a relationship, you have to accept that a part of you—the part that was born and only lived when you were with that person—is now dead and gone.

Well, the same goes for regrets. Finding closure for your regrets means letting your lost self die off once and for all. That death is necessary so you can learn what your regret is trying to teach you.

Here's the irony: at the 'Cocktail Party of You', the only version of you that can teach you something you don't already know is the 'Regrettable You'. It's the one version of yourself that can show you where your narratives have gone wrong, where your understanding of yourself has faltered, where you are refusing to take responsibility for your life and your pain.

We often hold onto our regrets as another way of avoiding responsibility. And confronting our 'Regrettable Self' makes that responsibility unavoidable—we have to face and accept who we really are. And that's probably going to hurt.

Regret can take us through a whole spectrum of emotional states. One side of the spectrum is the dark lament we feel when we're reminded of how fucked up and flawed we are. But the other side of regret, the side that makes it all worth it, is the light it shines in. That light guides us to a better understanding of ourselves—and ultimately to a place of acceptance of how flawed we are.

In the end, the slow burn of regret that carries on for years is really just a death by a thousand tiny cuts. So let your regrets turn into a raging wildfire that kills everything in its path.

CHAPTER 16

WHY YOU FEEL 'REGRET'– AND WHAT YOU CAN DO ABOUT IT?

If you look back over the course of your life, do you feel you took advantage of every opportunity that came your way? Or, are you living with the weight of regret? No matter how accomplished you may be, it's true that everyone experiences the harsh reality of knowing they failed to take action in pursuing something they wanted for themselves.

These are the inevitable realities of living a complex life, a life full of ups and downs. And perhaps, there's a small handful of people living regret-free lives. But for the vast majority of us, regret is a real thing that we have to face. So whether you bemoan doing something you wish you hadn't or miss doing something you wish you had, 'regret' is a universal emotion. The study of regret goes beyond just missed opportunities and regrettable actions. Recently, researchers have begun to explore the link between regret and a person's general self-concept. They have started asking questions as: Do you have a clear sense of who you are, and are you living up to the person you want to be? Are you living your life in a way that fulfills your duties and responsibilities to others?

These types of questions motivated a recent study. Scientists proposed that a person's most enduring regrets are more likely to stem from the discrepancies between actual and "ideal" selves, rather than between actual and "ought" selves. Put simply, you are much more likely to dwell on all you could have been than on all you should have been.

A closer look at self-discrepancy theory

The distinction between the 'could as' and the 'should as' is related to how you carve up your sense of self.

According to the psychologist Edward Higgins, a person's sense of self is made up of three components: 'actual, ideal and ought' selves.

The "actual self" is your own basic self-concept, your representation of the traits and qualities you believe you possess.

Your "ideal self" is the representation of attributes you would like to have ideally, be it related to your future goals, wishes, etc.

Lastly, your "ought self" is your representation of the qualities you believe you should possess, based on duties and obligations that are socially rooted.

When there is a discrepancy between any of these selves, a number of negative emotions are bound to arise. Specifically, emotions such as disappointment and sadness result from the belief that you are not living up to your "ideal" self. In contrast, if you believe you are failing to live up to your "ought" self, you are more likely to experience emotions such as guilt and fear.

Building on this theory, the researchers in the present investigation wanted to test two hypotheses. First, they predicted that people's most enduring regrets result more from the discrepancies between their actual and ideal selves than their actual and ought selves. Second, they wanted to discover the specific mechanism responsible for this difference. They suggested at the outset that the way you cope with regret affects its longevity in your life. Specifically, failures to live up to your "ought" self call for more immediate action and coping efforts to repair the damage. In contrast, failures to live up to your "ideal" self are perceived as less urgent and are often placed on a back burner, which in turn makes those regrets more enduring and detrimental in the long run.

Study and results

To test their hypotheses, the researchers conducted six separate studies. In the first study, they simply asked the participants which they regretted more—failing to live up to their 'ideal' selves or their 'ought' selves. In line with the predictions, the majority of participants reported experiencing more regret regarding not being the person they could have been.

In studies 2 and 3, the researchers asked the participants to recall specific, significant regrets they had experienced in their lives, and to indicate whether those regrets were more ideal or ought-based. Again, as predicted, participants were more likely to regret their failure to live up to their ideal selves.

Next, in studies 4 and 5, the researchers tested their second hypothesis: Are coping differences the reason for the increased weight of ideal-based regret? That is, the researchers predicted that participants would be more likely to attend to and deal with ought-related regrets than ideal-related regrets. That's exactly what they found. It seems then, that ought-related regrets require more immediate behavioral and psychological repair work, whereas ideal-related regrets seems as though they can be put away and dealt with at a later time. Part of this might be due to the pressures of impression management and the constant desire to be accepted by others.

The central aim of the sixth and final study was to uncover the link between resolved and unresolved regrets, and whether those regrets were related more to the participants' ideal selves or their ought selves.

Once again, the findings suggested that ideal-related regrets are less likely to elicit psychological and behavioral coping efforts, which leads people to think they are still unresolved. In contrast, because people have a more pressing need to deal with their ought-related regrets , they are more likely to ultimately perceive them as resolved and dealt with.

Why it matters for you and your life?

Contrary to what you hear in the media or what your friends tell you, living life without any regrets is pretty much an impossible task. It is completely natural to wonder what your life could have been like had you chosen another career path or had you married your high school sweetheart. From major life-altering decisions to trivial everyday choices—our lives are full of could haves and should haves. It's what makes us human.

Importantly , not all regrets are felt the same. They differ in number and intensity based on the different categories of self-concept. It all depends on who you are and what you are trying to achieve. If you define yourself more by your obligations and responsibilities (the "ought"), it would be wise to think carefully before making any decisions that involve close others in your life. On the other hand, if you are guided more by your personal ideal, then you may be happier deciding on the thing that move you closer to it.

The first step, then, in reducing regret: know thyself.

CHAPTER 17

HOW EXAMINING OUR 'REGRETS' CAN MAKE FOR A MORE MEANINGFUL LIFE?

Instead of living a life with no 'regrets', what if we embraced them? What if we used the past as a guide for better living?

That's what Daniel H. Pink asks us to consider, after spending years researching human regret — an emotion distinct from sadness or disappointment because of the agency involved in it.

A journalist and author of several non-fiction books, including **The Power of Regret: How Looking Backward Moves Us Forward**, Pink got curious about regret and decided to compile data on it in a qualitative way — he surveyed regret all over the world, asking anyone to write in with their regrets, ultimately receiving tens of thousands of stories and missives with which he could compile, classify, analyze and recognize patterns.

People regret not taking action

A key takeaway, he found, was that regrets of inaction outnumber regrets of action 2:1, and it goes up as people age. That's because "action" regrets, like marrying the wrong person, can be undone, and you can think about them in terms of "at leasts." For example, many people who felt they married the wrong person would say, "At least I have these great kids." With regrets of inaction, that's impossible.

Sponsor message

Pink said, "One of the big categories of regrets that you see are boldness regrets. If only I'd taken the chance. If only I'd asked out that person on a date. If only I traveled. If only I'd spoken up. If only I'd launched a business. We should have a bias for action because we overstate the amount of risk and difficulty sometimes. What's more, I think ... we plan too much and act too little. Sometimes we don't realize that action is a form of knowing. That we can figure stuff out by doing it."

Pink's data showed 'regrets' tend to cluster into four different types:

Foundation regrets: These are the regrets from not "doing the work." Not laying the foundation for a more stable, less precarious life. Things like, not saving money for retirement. Not getting a certain degree, not exercising and eating right to take good care of your body.

Moral regrets: Regrets in which you did the wrong thing. Bullying is an example, or choices of unkindness. "I was stunned by how many people regretted bullying people younger in their life, and marital infidelity," Pink said.

Connection regrets: "If only I'd reached out," is the sign of a connection regret. It is the largest category of regrets, and they are about relationships — family, friendships, romantic and beyond. These regrets come about when people drift apart, but neither tries to connect for fear it's awkward. Reaching out, Pink says, is "very rarely as awkward as people think, and it's almost always well-received."

Boldness regrets: Boldness regrets are about a chance that wasn't taken. Things like opportunities to study abroad or leaving a dead-end job, but for whatever reason, you chose to play it safe.

These four types of regrets revealed what humans value, Pink says. They have something to teach us. Pink uses the example of photographic negatives to explain how each of the most common regret types reveal, in their inverse, a deep human need. The human need for growth is linked to boldness regrets, for example. With moral regrets, the need is goodness. With foundation regrets, it's stability. And with connection regrets, the human need is love.

"Looking back can help us moving forward, but only if we do it right," he writes.

Doing regret right

So if we're not living a life without regrets, but instead maximizing our regrets to live a fuller, more flourishing life, how do we actually do that? Pink suggests a three-part strategy: inward, outward and forward.

1. **Look inward**: Reframe how we think about our regrets. We speak to ourselves more cruelly than we'd speak to anyone else. Practice self-compassion.
2. **Look outward**: Practice disclosure. Sharing your emotions is a form of unburdening. We can make sense of regret through talking or writing.
3. **Move forward**: Extract a lesson from your regret. You need to create distance to help yourself process.

Some ideas:

- Talk to yourself in the third person. "What should Dan do?"
- Imagine making a phone call to yourself in 10 years. Ask yourself about your choice, "Should I buy a blue car or a green car?" You'll quickly see that the future you doesn't care. "Should I go to this funeral or reach out to a friend?"
- Ask yourself: what advice would I give my best friend?

Exercises to help you 'optimize' regret

"Our goal should not be to minimize regret. It should be to optimize it," Pink writes. So in addition to the "inward, outward, forward" system, he also offers some fun, practical ways to work regrets into living more fully.

For example, we all have resumes full of our accomplishments. What about a failure resume? This is an idea he credits to Tina Seeling. It's a way to metabolize our past missteps by putting them in writing.

Or combining our annual New Year's Resolutions with last year's regrets, so that the feeling of regret can be used for thinking and reflection, and that reflection can then power action.

Because a relentless drive forward, a relentless posture of happiness, does not make for a full life. "Americans have been sold a bill of goods that we should be positive all the time, that we should always look forward," Pink says. "There's a reason we experience negative emotions. They're useful if we treat them right. Regret, you don't want to wallow in it. You don't want to ruminate over it. But if you think of it as a signal, as information, as a knock at the door, it is a powerfully transformative emotion."

Looking backward can point us to a fuller, more meaningful life.

CHAPTER 18

THE STORY OF 'REGRET'?

There was this guy who believed very much in true love and decided to take his time to wait for his right girl to appear. He believed that there would definitely be someone special out there for him, but none came. Every year at Christmas, his ex-girlfriend would return from Vancouver to look him up. He was aware that she still held some hope of re-kindling the past romance with him. He did not wish to mislead her in any way. So he would always get one of his girl friends to pose as his steady whenever she came back. That went on for several years and each year, the guy would get a different girl to pose as his romantic interest.

So whenever the ex-girlfriend came to visit him, she would be led into believing that it was all over between her and the guy. The girl took all those rather well, often trying to casually tease him about his different girlfriends, or so, as it seemed! In fact, the girl often wept in secret whenever she saw him with another girl, but she was too proud to admit it. Still, every Christmas, she returned, hoping to re-kindle some form of romance. But each time, she returned to Vancouver feeling disappointed.

Finally, she decided that she could not play that game any longer. Therefore, she confronted him and professed that after all those years, he was still the only man that she had ever loved. Although the guy knew of her feelings for him, he was still taken back and have never expected her to react that way. He always thought that she would slowly forget about him over time and come to terms that it was all over between them. Although he was touched by her undying love for him and wanted so much to accept her again, he remembered why he rejected her in the first place-she was not the one he wanted. So he hardened his heart and turned her down cruelly. Since then, three years have passed and the girl never returned anymore. They never even wrote to each other. The guy went on with his life... still searching for the one but somehow deep inside him, he missed the girl.

On the Christmas of 1995, he went to his friend's party alone. "Hey, how come all alone this year? Where are all your girlfriends? What happened to that Vancouver babe who joins you every Christmas?", asked one of his friends. He felt warm and comforted by his friend's queries about her still, he just surged on.

Then, he came upon one of his many girlfriends whom he once requested to pose as his steady. He wanted so much to ignore her ..... not that he was impolite, but because at that moment, he just didn't feel comfortable with those girlfriends anymore. It was almost like he was being judged by them. The girl saw him and shouted across the floor for him. Unable to avoid her, he went up to acknowledge her.

"Hi... how are you? Enjoying the party?" the girl asked.

"Sure... yeah!", he replied.

She was slightly tipsy... must be from the whiskey on her hand. She continued, "Why? Don't you need someone to pose as your girlfriend this year?" Then he answered, "No, there is no need for that anymore."

Before he could continue, he was interrupted, "Oh yes! Must have found a girlfriend! You haven't been searching for one for the past years, right?" The man looked up as if he has struck gold, his face beamed and looked directly at the drunken girl. He replied, "Yes... you are right! I haven't been looking for anyone for the past years."

With that, the man darted across the floor and out the door, leaving the lady in much bewilderment. He finally realized that he has already found his dream girl, and she was... the Vancouver girl all along! The drunken lady has said something that awoken him.

All along he had found his girl. That was why he did not bother to look further when he realized she was not coming back. It was not any specific girl he was seeking! It was the perfection that he wanted, and yes... perfection!

A Relationship is something both parties should work on. Realizing that he had let away someone so important in his life, he decided to call her immediately. His whole mind was flooded with fear. He was afraid that she might have found someone new or no longer had the same feelings anymore... For once, he felt the fear of losing someone.

As it was Christmas eve, the line was quite hard to get through, especially an overseas call. He tried again and again, never giving up. Finally, he got through.... precisely at 1200 midnight. He confessed his love for her and the girl was moved to tears. It seemed that she never got over him! Even after so long, she was still waiting for him, never giving up.

He was so excited to meet her and to begin his new chapter of their lives. He decided to fly to Vancouver to join her. It was the happiest time of their lives! But their happy time was short-lived. Two days before he was supposed to fly to Vancouver, he received a call from her father. She had a head-on car collision with a drunken driver. She passed away after 6 hours in a coma.

The guy was devastated, as it was a complete loss. Why did fate play such cruel games with him? He cursed the heaven for taking her away from him, denying even one last look at her! How cruel he cursed! How he damned the Gods...!! How he hated himself... for taking so long to realize his mistake!! That was in 1996.

Moral: Treasure what you have...time is too slow for those who wait, too swift for those who fear, too long for those who grief, too short for those who rejoice, But for those who love... Time is Eternity. For all you out there with someone special in your heart, cherish that person, cherish every moment that you spend together that special someone, for in life, anything can happen anytime. You may painfully regret, only to realize that it is too late.

Source: Moralstories.org

https://www.moralstories.org › story-of-regret

CHAPTER 19

MANAGING 'REGRET AND GUILT' WHEN YOU REALLY HURT SOMEONE

Mistakes make us feel terrible. Guilt and remorse are two emotions that typically follow making mistakes. They carry with them a lot of emotional distress impacting our ability to move on from bad outcomes.

Other people will often try to make us feel better when we make mistakes. Saying: "It was no big deal" is one way people try to alleviate our pain from making mistakes. "This too shall pass" is another way people try to help us recognize that the negative impact of what happened will end eventually. Pointing out how we may not be the only ones responsible for a mistake can also be a way of trying to help us feel better.

But what if your mistake was a big deal? And what if the mistake was one that will have major repercussions for a long time and was one that was clearly all your fault? What do you do then?

I see people in therapy all the time facing this dilemma. They know they messed up and know that what they did hurt others. It may have been a bad business decision, ignoring a regulation that should not have been ignored, or not keeping close enough watch on a child. It may also have been engaging in an affair or revealing a secret that was never meant to be shared. When clients come in with these problems they know they did something wrong and that they hurt others. They are not looking to be talked out of feeling responsible, but they do want to know what to do with the pain.

If you think of this from our animal nature, why we feel so strongly after major mistakes can seem obvious. Animals are hard-wired to react strongly to error, this prevents them from making the mistake again. Animals out in the wild, with whom we share a lot of the same behavioral patterns, cannot afford to make major mistakes. Turn the wrong way when trying to escape a lion and you become lunch .

That is the more obvious explanation for why mistakes impact us so much. But it does not say anything about how animals deal with mistakes. Animals respond quickly to mistakes as a way of avoiding them. But how exactly they respond can tell us even more about how we can handle major mistakes effectively.

Non-human animals, for instance, do not dwell on mistakes. They do not ignore them but do not dwell on them. When animals lose a battle, often due to mistakes like misjudging an opponent , they accept what happened and move on as best they can. It would not be correct to say that they ignore the mistake but, rather, they incorporate the mistake and loss into how they move on in the future. Staying "future-focused" helps animals keep their eyes open on doing what they can to make things better despite what just happened.

Behavioral research on mice also can give us a different way of looking at regret. In a study of mice and mistakes **Sweis, Brian, Thomas and Redish (2018)** found evidence that "regret" in the animal world is associated more with making a mistake a second time. When mice made mistakes for finding food they were not clearly impacted by the mistake other than taking steps to not make those mistakes again. In other words, "regret" was associated with not learning from mistakes.

And then, there is the study of "guilt" for non-human animals. There have not been many such studies but one **(Horowitz, 2009)** found that dogs tended to show signs of "feeling guilty" primarily in response to how their owners acted. What was interpreted as dogs feeling guilt was actually a response to external cues. Research like this supports that guilt often comes about by perception of how others respond to mistakes.

The results of comparative psychology research across species on guilt and remorse support some good suggestions for how to deal with our mistakes:

- Own up to your mistakes and do not hide from them. Allow yourself to feel bad but also remind yourself that the only way you are going to make things better is to focus on moving forward.
- Try to "live in the moment". Admit to yourself and others what you did and find every way you can to make things better. Focus on what you can do "right now" to make things better. That includes finding ways to make up for problems your mistakes caused.
- Make clear to yourself and others that you are doing everything possible to learn from your mistakes.
- Use clear statements to those you hurt showing that you know what you did, how it impacted them, and how you will have to face the consequences. The more direct you are with others the more direct they will be about what they expect from you moving forward.
- If you feel "stuck," be direct about that feeling to those you hurt. Even if they do not know what specifically they expect from you it is still better to show you are trying to find a path forward.

Sadness and anger at ourselves when we do things that really and severely hurt others are natural responses. But allowing them to keep you from moving forward and improving things is not only going to hurt you but is also likely to make life more difficult for those you already hurt.

CHAPTER 20

QUOTES ABOUT 'FORGIVENESS' THAT WILL INSPIRE YOU TO MOVE ON

All of us have experienced the deep cuts that go along with being hurt by someone else, emotionally or physically. When that kind of personal affront takes place, it's easy to grab onto that pain and suffering and let those wounds fester. But eventually, we become so beaten down by the family drama, workplace tension, toxic friendships, broken heart, past regret, or whatever else it is that is taking up precious space in our minds and hearts.

That's where these forgiveness quotes come in. It takes a lot of grace, mental strength and courage to practice forgiveness—either toward the person who has wronged you or to yourself. While you may never forget how you were hurt, by forgiving, you are taking steps toward healing yourself—spiritually, emotionally and mentally.

1. "Forgiveness is a funny thing. It warms the heart and cools the sting." — William A. Ward
2. "We must develop and maintain the capacity to forgive. He who is devoid of the power to forgive is devoid of the power to love." —

Martin Luther King, Jr., A Gift of Love

3. "Never forget the three powerful resources you always have available to you: love, prayer, and forgiveness." — H. Jackson Brown, Jr.
4. "Never does the human soul appear so strong as when it foregoes revenge." — Edward Hubbell Chapin
5. "The stupid neither forgive nor forget; the naive forgive and forget; the wise forgive but do not forget." — Thomas Szasz
6. "It's not an easy journey, to get to a place where you forgive people. But it is such a powerful place because it frees you." — Tyler Perry
7. "It's one of the greatest gifts you can give yourself, to forgive. Forgive everybody." — Maya Angelou
8. "If we really want to love, we must learn how to forgive." — Mother Teresa
9. "Always forgive your enemies; nothing annoys them so much." — Oscar Wilde
10. "How unhappy is he who cannot forgive himself." — Publilius Syrus

*****

www.ingramcontent.com/pod-product-compliance
Ingram Content Group UK Ltd.
Pitfield, Milton Keynes, MK11 3LW, UK
UKHW042012190726
13854UKWH00005B/2265